Spirit Energy:

Table tipping, trumpet voices, trance channeling and other phenomena of physical mediumship

Other books by the author

The Awesomely Amazing Adventures of Cherry: Butterfly Buddies

Intuitive Symbols Coloring Book: Unlock your intuition through meditative coloring

The Spiritual Symbols Workbook: Create your personal dictionary of intuitive, psychic and metaphysical symbols

Led by Light: How to develop your intuitive mediumship abilities, Book One

Led by Light: A medium's guide to developing your intuitive and psychic senses, Book Two

My Signs from Spirit Journal: Communicate with your intuition, guides and loved ones in Spirit through signs and symbols in your everyday life

Spirit Energy:

Table tipping, trumpet voices, trance channeling and other phenomena of physical mediumship

Rev. Joanna Bartlett

Publisher's Cataloging-in-Publication Data

Names: Bartlett, Joanna, author.
Title: Spirit energy : table tipping, trumpet voices, trance channeling and other phenomena of physical mediumship / Rev. Joanna Bartlett.
Description: Eugene, OR : Alight Press, 2018. | Previously published by Alight Press in 2017 as part of Led by Light, bk. 2.
Identifiers: LCCN 2018901755 | ISBN 978-1-945489-11-2 (pbk.) | ISBN 978-1-945489-13-6 (ebook)
Subjects: LCSH: Mediums. | Channeling (Spiritualism) | Table-moving (Spiritualism) | Spiritualism. | Occultism. | Supernatural. | BISAC: BODY, MIND & SPIRIT / Channeling & Mediumship. | BODY, MIND & SPIRIT / Parapsychology / ESP (Clairvoyance, Precognition, Telepathy) | BODY, MIND & SPIRIT / Spiritualism. | BODY, MIND & SPIRIT / Supernatural.
Classification: LCC BF1286 .B37 2018 (print) | LCC BF1286 (ebook) | DDC 133.9/1--dc23.

Alight Press LLC
2075 Charnelton St.
Eugene, OR 97405
www.alightpress.com

Printed in the United States of America

Contents

Introduction

Physical mediumship is a Spiritualist phenomenon that holds a lot of mystery and conflicting information.

For some people, it's a fascinating facet of mediumship: actual, tangible evidence that the laws of physics and the workings of the world may not be exactly as they seem.

For others, it seems it must all be fakery.

Given that many forms of physical mediumship are performed in dark or dimly-lit rooms and the explanations of how they work are shrouded in secrecy and confusing explanations, it's not surprising there are conflicting views.

This book aims to clear up much of the mystery, conflict and secrecy.

While I'm definitely not an expert on physical mediumship, I have studied, worked with, experienced and produced several forms of physical mediumship in the 17 years since I began studying mediumship in 2001. Between that, my research, and tapping into my own intuition for guidance, what follows is my understanding of how physical mediumship works overall, along with each of its phases, and the steps you can take to learn how to do it yourself, if you so desire.

I also want to say upfront that I realize I may not have all the right answers. There are things I may be misunderstanding myself.

In this book, I explain physical mediumship to the best of my ability, based on my experiences, research and current understanding. If it makes sense to you, that's great. If you think it works differently, that's fine, too.

Some of the concepts and ideas seem a bit out there, I admit, and contradictory information abounds in terms of how it works and how to do it (what lighting is necessary, for instance).

I encourage you to think critically, with an open mind, and a sense of possibility. There are so many things in this world that, until we had the science and the language to explain them, seemed inexplicable. Imagine someone 50 years ago trying to explain how your cell phone works, before we had the ability to produce tiny, powerful computers capable of the processing powers of today's cell phones. Or think about how the concept of electricity, something we understand well and completely take for granted, would have seemed to people in the 17th century. They knew about static electricity from friction and electric fish, but not the true power of what it could accomplish and how it worked. My sense is that a lot of how mediumship works, mental and physical, is similar—we just don't have the concepts and vocabulary for science to quantify it yet.

I've consulted with several texts on physical mediumship to give you as accurate and thorough an explanation and understanding of the phenomenon as a I can. I hope this book is useful to you and helpful in your journey for knowledge end experience in Spiritualist physical mediumship.

An overview of physical mediumship

Physical mediumship is a fascinating facet of mediumship.

For some people, it feels more solid and real than mental mediumship, as you can see the phenomena happening with your eyes, or hear it with your physical ears, and it can usually be confirmed and observed by others present.

Forms of physical mediumship include:

- Rapping, table tipping and levitation
- Materialization, etherealization and transfiguration
- Apportation
- Precipitation
- Direct voice and trumpet mediumship
- Automatic writing and drawing, including planchette
- Independent writing and slate writing
- Trance channeling

- Spirit photography
- Spoon bending
- Dowsing and pendulum work

Many phases of physical mediumship—specifically the ectoplasm-based ones including levitation, materialization, direct voice and spirit photography—aren't practiced like they used to be in Spiritualism's heyday and finding practitioners can be difficult in the United States. However, other forms are practiced widely—trance channeling and pendulum work, for instance—even if many practitioners don't consider them to be physical mediumship.

I don't know for sure why the ectoplasm-based phases of mediumship have fallen out of favor but, from talking to fellow mediums and Spirit, I have some theories:

- **We've moved beyond it**

  We no longer need the concrete, tangible connection with Spirit that is apparent in many forms of physical mediumship. We have so many wise people stepping forward who are explaining how the universe works in words and ideas, rather than having Spirit move physical objects around a room. Most people now believe in life after death and that personal identity, in one form or another, continues on after a person's physical body dies. According to the Pew Research Center's 2014 Religious Landscape Study, 72 percent of people believe in an afterlife. We don't need to prove that Spirit exists because we already believe life continues on.

- **Its popularity may have been its very downfall**
  As M. H. and E. W. Wallis write in *A Guide to Mediumship and Psychical Unfoldment*, "It is impossible for a medium, or for the spirits, to satisfy *all* the whims and demands of skeptical and cynical sitters, or to gratify the wishes of those who are always on the lookout for 'something new and strange.' They cannot produce phenomena on demand; or turn on the tap and let the forces flow like water." (p. 195)
- **Fraud put people off**
  There was some fraud at the height of physical mediumship due to pressures to perform and, potentially, make a living. Unfortunately, this led to increased skepticism, which basically

makes it extremely difficult, if not impossible, to produce the phenomena.

As Jefts writes in *The Laws of Spirit Mediumship,* "Thoughts are real and active things. A doubt vibration makes conditions that are most impossible for the Spirit Forces to puncture...No matter how strong the Medium may be, the thoughts of the sitters can, to a certain extent, make or mar a séance. One person can throw out doubt vibrations strong enough to spoil a large circle." (p. 20-21)

- **We're too impatient**

  It takes a lot of time to develop physical mediumship and few people are willing to sit for the required time it can take to develop successfully. While I realize every generation makes derisive comments about wherewithal, abilities and patience (or lack of) of the generation that comes after them, it does seem that, on the whole, students want quick results. Few of us, including me, like the idea of sitting for months, if not years, before producing physical phenomena.

- **We need special circles to develop it**

  Not only does it take time to develop physical

mediumship skills, it takes other mediums. It's not a solitary activity. Most often, developing mediums work and practice in home circles. So you'd need a home circle dedicated to developing physical mediumship abilities. According to the Wallis' "The present dearth of physical phenomena is directly due to the abandonment of the practice of holding home circles...The existence of the psychical sensitiveness upon which mediumship depends can best be discovered, aroused, and regulated in the 'spirit circle.' The home circle has been the nursery of most mediums of note." (*A Guide to Mediumship*, p. 37)

How physical mediumship works

Physical mediumship is different from mental mediumship in that mental mediumship comes primarily through your mind and physical mediumship goes through your body.

While some aspects of mental mediumship, such as clairsentience, can feel quite physical and use your intuitive body and its energy centers to receive and information, it's the connection with your brain that interprets the information and makes sense of it. Your ears may be a physical feature that hear sound-waves, but your brain interprets them into meaning, whether that's the sound of a word, a baby's cry or a bird call. Even clairsentience and the push and pull of energy or the seeming physical sensations of how someone died aren't truly physical.

In physical mediumship, the manifestations themselves are usually of a physical nature, which can be independently and objectively observed—such as a table tipping, direct voice and materialization—or they come through the physical body without using the medium's mental faculties to make them occur—such as automatic writing and trance channeling.

To produce physical mediumship, the medium's physical body needs to be a good conduit for these physical manifestations.

What makes a good physical conduit? According to Clifford Bias in his booklet *Physical Mediumship*, there needs to be "a plentiful source of etheric energy," which is furnished by the sitters and the medium that the medium is then able to make available for the Spirit entities to use to produce physical phenomena.

Bias suggests that a medium can test whether or not they might have a plentiful supply of etheric energy by doing some light exercises, raising up and down on their toes several times, then bending backward and forward with their hands on their hips until they experience a "glow" or feeling of exhilaration. At that point, while standing in front of a mirror in a dimly lit room, they can rub their hands together, press their fingertips together, then draw them apart, watching their reflection in the mirror.

"A 'stream' of etheric substance can be seen (if you have a superabundance of it) connecting the fingers," Bias writes. It will be barely visible and faint electric blue or peach in color. (*Physical Mediumship*, p. 11)

Ectoplasm

If you've studied physical mediumship at all, you've probably heard of ectoplasm—the mysterious substance that makes it possible.

The reason that having lots of etheric energy is important in physical mediumship is because it's used to produce ectoplasm.

Bias described ectoplasm as "a semi-physical, semi-etheric substance" that is actually "'physicalized' etheric matter." (*Physical Mediumship*, p. 14)

In *Mediumship and Its Phases*, Margaret L. King describes ectoplasm as "matter invisible and intangible in its primary state but assuming vaporous, liquid or solid condition in its various stages of condensation." (p. 31)

Bias agrees that ectoplasm can vary in appearance and density—it can be invisible, a misty gas, a "viscous gelatin like fluid," a soft lacy material or a hard solid. (*Physical Mediumship*, p. 14) I've also heard it described as Spirit snot, as it's often mucousy.

In color, Bias says it's usually pale—white, grey or pastel—although sometimes back, but rarely a bright color.

The word *ectoplasm* was coined by Charles Richet, a French physiologist, in 1894.

Physical mediums exude etheric energy and ectoplasm from their solar plexus and orifices (yes, all of them) which is then used by Spirit to form the supports that move tables around, levitate people, create voice boxes for trumpet mediumship, and materialize as the face of a loved one in Spirit, etc.

When practicing physical mediumship, ectoplasm and etheric energy comes not only from the medium, but from everyone present. Some people say that the medium's doctor or chemist Spirit guide uses the etheric energy to alter the chemistry of the medium's body to produce ectoplasm. However, if your belief is (like mine) that your Spirit guides are really aspects of your own higher self, rather than separate entities, then it's your own inner wisdom making any such changes to produce ectoplasm, rather than an external force.

Generally, the dominant physical medium in the group not only produces etheric energy, but draws energy from the other sitters, centers it within themselves and turns it into ectoplasm for Spirit to then produce physical phenomena with. The precise method of how this happens seems unknown.

A Spirit control

The other aspect of physical mediumship is working with an entity in Spirit, who understands how to manipulate the ectoplasm produced by the medium and sitters, and how to turn it into physical manifestations of whatever sort.

What kind of Spirit control are you likely to get as you develop physical mediumship? Well, just as with mental mediumship, the laws of vibration and attraction come into play. This means you're going to attract someone in Spirit who is harmonious with you and has an affinity for your energy.

How to develop physical mediumship

If physical mediumship is something you're drawn to, and you have the time, energy and patience to develop it, then go for it.

Develop mental mediumship first

Many books recommend developing mental mediumship first, before exploring physical mediumship. This is wise. By having an already established and developed relationship with your guides and open and working intuitive senses, you'll be able to receive the needed instruction more easily from the Spirits who will step in to help you with physical mediumship.

Working with physical mediumship, especially the phenomena that require the medium to go into a trance state and/or produce ectoplasm, is a partnership between you and those in Spirit. You need to be able to receive and understand the instructions and fine tuning that you'll get from those in Spirit to help make the phenomena occur.

Find or start a development circle

Once you feel sufficiently capable of whichever phases of mental mediumship work well for you, find or start a physical mediumship development circle. If you're already part of a circle to develop your mental mediumship abilities, you'll likely need a separate one to sit for physical mediumship. That's because you want everyone in the circle to be willing and open to develop physical mediumship and experience physical phenomena. Some people are either not up for that, not interested in it, or not patient enough to stick around, week in and week out, until it happens.

How do you find people interested in developing physical mediumship abilities? If there's a Spiritualist or metaphysical church in your area, you might find one already in existence or people willing to be part of one. Otherwise, as of this writing at least, Meetup.com is a good resource to connect with people in your geographic area with similar interests. You can search for people and groups in your area, or you can start a Meetup group of your own.

Once you do find like-minded and like-hearted folks with the same intentions as you, make the circle a closed circle. This means you don't let just anyone show up each week. Your circle should have the same people each time you meet.

This does a couple of things. It keeps the energy consistent and it allows the circle members to feel comfortable and secure with each other. Any kind of mediumship takes trust, physical mediumship especially. It's new territory for many people. You want to do it with people you feel good about.

Of course, people will be absent from time to time, but you want there to be a commitment and consistent attendance. What I've found in development circles and even classes that span a number of weeks is that, even when a member is absent, you can feel their energy there. They're still connected to the circle or class.

This doesn't mean you can't ever invite a new person into the circle. That's fine, as long as you have the agreement of the other members. But aim for consistent attendance by the same group of people for the best results.

The seance room

Often, physical mediumship is practiced in a room specially made for that purpose, and usually called a séance room. That sounds much spookier than it actually is.

A séance room is, essentially, the room you dedicate to working with physical mediumship. If you can somehow dedicate a small room for this work, that's wonderful. Keep it clean and sparse, if you can. If you can't use a separate room, then cleanse the energy every so often to keep it clear. And declutter as much as you can.

Some people say you should paint your séance room entirely in matte black and make sure no cracks of light can get in—and I've sat in séances where we had a completely black room. I don't think it's necessary and have seen and produced physical phenomena in my living room, with lamplight from the streetlamps coming in through the windows and my kids sleeping upstairs.

Clifford Bias has some very specific instructions in his guide, *Physical Mediumship*, one of which is to paint the walls and ceiling flat white. He also stresses the importance of a light-sealed room and the use of a red light, and recommends the room be rectangular, have a dark-carpeted, squeak-free floor, comfortable chairs, little furniture and enough entrances and exits in case of an emergency. (p. 34)

The insistence on darkness is to help the ectoplasm form and coalesce and many physical mediums believe it is impeded in doing this if there is light present.

However, in *A Guide to Mediumship and Psychical Unfoldment,* Wallis reports that Daniel Dunglas Home, a well-known levitator during his time, insisted that "the phenomena could be got just as well in the light, and even if some of the things were not so strong, the evidence of one's eyesight was worth making some sacrifices for." (p. 54)

There doesn't seem to be a definitive answer here, so perhaps try different things and see what works for you. What I can say is that I've been in circles and demonstrations in my own home, friends' homes, churches and even hotel ballrooms that have successfully produced visible phenomena without total darkness or a special room.

In terms of lighting whatever room you're using, a red light is widely considered to be the best way to view the phenomena without causing the ectoplasm to dissipate or shrink.

Setting expectations

Don't expect every séance to be a success or be disappointed if little or nothing occurs, advises Wallis in *A Guide to Mediumship and Psychical Unfoldment.* Rather, "sometimes a 'good failure' is as helpful and as educational as a 'grand success,' if the members of the circle are thoughtful and observant and endeavor to ascertain the causes of the *non*-success." (p. 112)

What I've found is that, while you're sitting for physical mediumship, whether or not anything actually seems to occur, you'll receive instructions and information from Spirit and your guides and higher self on what to do next. You just have to be willing to listen. This is why developing your mental intuitive mediumship abilities first is so helpful.

Some teachers, such as the Wallises, feel it's not needed to even give instructions about the different types of physical phenomena that use ectoplasm because "those mediums who possess the psycho-physical qualifications for these demonstrations almost invariably elaborate strong and abundant psychic force by means of which the spirits themselves can give instructions...how the seances are to be conducted." (*A Guide to Mediumship*, p. 194)

For most of us, though, instructions can be helpful. In the following chapters, I'll share everything I know about the different phases of physical mediumship and how to best prepare for and produce them. However, keep in mind that you may get your own instructions from Spirit and your guides about the specifics and particulars as you further your own development.

This goes back to trusting yourself and your connection with Spirit. Be open to what your guides and your Spirit control have to tell you and give different things a try, staying in a sense of wonder and delighted expectation.

Considerations

Is physical mediumship safe to practice? Generally, yes. Some things to keep in mind are:

It takes energy to produce phenomena

Because physical mediumship is produced using etheric energy from the medium's and sitters' physical bodies, there can be an energy drain associated with it, much like there is with any physical activity. That doesn't necessarily mean it's harmful—just like going on a five-mile jog isn't harmful if your body is conditioned to it. But it does mean it can have an effect on your physical self.

So go slowly. Don't start running the equivalent of five miles your first time, even if you get phenomena right away. Go easy. Build up your strength and understanding.

It's also important to take good care of your physical body if you're going to do physical mediumship. Otherwise, it's hard on your body and makes regular life a lot less pleasant.

While I have only anecdotal evidence of this, most physical mediums that I've observed tend to either be overweight or have physical difficulties or infirmities. This may not be directly caused by physical mediumship, but my intuition tells me that it is. The reason I think this is so is because, when you give a lot of your awareness to energy outside of your physical self—whether that's connecting with loved ones in Spirit or producing physical phenomena—your body tends to ground you and remind you that it needs to be taken care of. It can do this by physically becoming heavier (which can also give you more substance with which to produce etheric energy) and by being loud and trying to get your attention through pain.

That's not to say you can't be a wonderful physical medium while being slender, in great shape and full of energy. You can. It's totally possible. But it does mean you need to learn to balance the energies, understand and listen to your body and its signals, and nurture and nourish yourself.

It takes time to produce phenomena

Most physical phenomena—especially ectoplasmic-based phenomena—takes time to produce. While it's helpful to read about what to expect, how you can set the stage for your development and what you might feel as the phenomena is occurring, there's no substitute for practice and experience.

Some groups or circles sitting for physical phenomena work on it for weeks, months, or even years before anything really happens.

Most of us don't have that kind of patience. If that's the case for you, give pendulum dowsing and spoon bending a try, as I've found them to be the easiest forms of physical mediumship, followed by rapping and table tipping.

It can be painful if you're interrupted

If you're going to practice physical mediumship, you need to make sure the space you're in is secure from disruption. Getting interrupted during a regular meditation for message work is annoying and sometimes mildly uncomfortable if your sense of self gets pulled back into your physical awareness unexpectedly. That discomfort multiplies with an interruption during physical mediumship.

As Jefts writes in *The Laws of Spirit Mediumship*, "Should someone touch a Spirit unexpectedly, flash a sudden light or startle the medium in any way, it might result in serious injury or perhaps even death to the instrument, through the nervous shock and the rapid recoil of the ectoplasm back into his body." (p. 26)

Bias isn't quite as dire, but does issue a warning against the medium being exposed to bright white or yellow light when they have extruded a significant amount of ectoplasm from their body, "for the sudden light causes the ectoplasm to snap back into the medium's body, causing shock and pain similar to a heavy blow." (*Physical Mediumship*, p. 14-15)

So perhaps not sudden death, should you be interrupted, but certainly unpleasant.

You also want to allow a little time at the end of a session for all the ectoplasm produced to go back into its respective bodies before you turn on the lights.

With these considerations in mind, if you haven't closed the book and run screaming, let's delve into the world of physical mediumship's different phases.

Rapping, table tipping and levitation

We'll start our exploration of the different phases of physical mediumship with one I'm familiar with and have practiced myself: table tipping.

Bias considered table tipping, also known as table tilting and table turning, to be one of the easier forms of physical mediumship as he feels it's less complicated. It's often considered to be a form of parakenesis—the movement of objects in contact with the medium.

Table tipping, rapping and levitation are lumped together because they use similar techniques to produce and the phenomena is created the same way. You can think of them as deepening levels of the same abilities—first comes rapping, which is easier for most people to produce, then table tipping, which requires more experience and physical mediumship abilities but isn't substantially difficult, then levitation of objects and people, which is the most advanced ability in this form of physical mediumship.

Rapping

Spirit raps are considered to be one of the earliest known phenomena of modern Spiritualism. Spiritualist history teaches that in Hydesville, New York, in 1848 the Fox family experienced raps and other phenomena in their cottage. Mrs. Fox tried to explain it away, but the phenomena continued and got stronger. "Furniture was moved, the touch of a cold hand was felt, and footsteps walking through the hallway and down the staircase to the cellar were heard." (Lesson 2, Morris Pratt Educational Course on Modern Spiritualism)

The family investigated the cause of the rapping, but couldn't find one. Finally, on March 31, 1848, two of the Fox sisters, Catherine and Margaretta—who were, I believe, 14 and 12 at the time—began making similar sounds to the raps by snapping their fingers. Catherine, said, "Mr. Splitfoot, do as I do," and began clapping her hands. The rapping imitated her in the number of raps it produced.

Mrs. Fox took over and began questioning the maker of the noises, asking it to produce two raps for a "yes" answer and also using the letters of the alphabet and their corresponding number of raps—1 for A,

7 for G, 15 for O, etc.—to obtain information from the entity. Through these raps, he communicated that his name was Charles Rosna and he'd been a 31-year-old peddler, murdered and buried in the cellar of the house.

And so began the advent of modern Spiritualism.

I've experienced rapping myself, although with no sinister story behind it.

I come by metaphysical and healing work honestly. My maternal grandfather was a healer—first as an herbalist, then later as a metaphysical healer through the church of Christian Science. He founded a church in his town of Pau, France, and did his best to impose the teachings on his five children. It didn't take for my mum, but two of her older brothers became steeped in the religion and were an active part of the church.

I didn't expect to follow in their footsteps in any way and it was surprising, even to me, that I embarked on becoming a Spiritualist minister. I felt a push from Spirit—and quite possibly, from my grandpa and uncle who were both in Spirit at that time.

The night I got my first lesson from the Morris Pratt Institute—the National Spiritualist Association's educational body—I was home on my own. I sat down at my computer to answer the first lesson's questions and was interrupted by knocking all around me.

At first, I thought it was the front door, or my office door, but it was coming from the walls and everywhere. I'll admit, it was a bit spooky.

After my initial fright, I thought to ask who it was, and got the strong impression of my uncle and grandpa, happy and celebrating my start on this new journey. They wanted to let me know they approved and were behind me all the way. Spiritualism is a different religion than Christian Science, although with a similar metaphysical basis, and I think they were pleased I was interested in learning more about how the universe works and expanding my spiritual self.

I couldn't concentrate with all the rapping going on, so I asked them to stop, which they did. I didn't have the presence of mind to attempt to communicate with them further through rapping. I felt I got the emotional message—the love and support they wanted to impart—and that was enough. So I got on with my course work.

How to produce rapping

Strangely, none of the books or sources I've read explain how to purposefully produce rapping phenomena as a standalone form of mediumship. The Spirit raps in my own experience have occurred randomly—such as in the event with my grandpa and uncle.

Raps are often produced when doing table tipping or direct voice/trumpet mediumship work as an early stage of the phenomena.

If you want to work on producing Spirit rapping and connecting with Spirit in this way, I suggest trying the following steps. You can do this in a group or alone, although you'll have more energy available in a group.

- Set your intention for your highest good and open your hatch or connection with Spirit.
- Allow yourself to go into a deep meditative state.
- Focus your awareness on your solar plexus and the energy that resides there.

- Ask your doctor guide to step in and assist in turning your etheric energy into ectoplasm that can be used by Spirit, if needed (I don't think this is always the case with rapping).
- Ask if there are any people in Spirit who would like to step in to communicate with you in this way.
- Once you hear some rapping or knocking, establish a key or code for the raps. A commonly used code, according to Bias, is one rap for "No," two raps for "Doubtful," three raps for "Yes," four raps for "Don't know," and five raps to call for spelling out the letters of the alphabet. In the case of spelling out the alphabet, someone in the circle says each letter with a short pause in between until a rap is heard, at which point someone writes down the letter, slowly revealing a message.

Table tipping

Table tipping used to be a popular way to manifest physical Spiritualist phenomena. I consider it to be a fun way to connect with Spirit and expand your mind and acceptance of what may be possible.

There are several theories about how table tipping actually works.

Rods made of ectoplasm is a common theory. King writes in *Mediumship and Its Phases* that "ectoplasm rods are formed in sufficient strength for spirit forces to bring about the rapping or table tipping." (p. 31) Bias considers the movement to be caused by the etheric energy of those present.

Skeptics say that it's really the unconscious minds of the sitters at work, causing small movements in the muscles of their hands and arms that make the table move. This is caused by the ideomotor response, which I'll cover more in the chapter on dowsing and pendulums.

Bias agrees that this can be case, as "the dominant or most active mind in the room, either incarnate or discarnate, can direct the motions of the table." (*Physical Mediumship*, p. 14) This most active mind can be that of someone in Spirit. But, if you don't know how to connect with Spirit, then it could possibly be "the conscious or unconscious desire of one or more of those present." That's why you should develop mental mediumship abilities first, so you can connect with Spirit.

In my own experience, I've seen the table move more than seems reasonable if it were just the sitters at work, consciously or not. I've even taken video of it and asked the sitters to move their hands so that you can clearly see that no one is actually moving the table.

There have also been reports of tables being tilted on two or one legs and even climbing the walls and levitating, which seems more of a stretch to believe is caused by our own unconscious desires than it is to believe it's Spirit at work.

How to practice table tipping

While some mediums can produce table tipping phenomena alone, as a beginner, you need the combined energy of several people. So, get together a small group of four to six people interested in learning about table tipping and willing to sit for, potentially, several weeks before anything exciting happens.

The table

Next, you need a table. Many sources suggest a small, round, three-legged wooden table. In my experience, it doesn't have to be any of those things, except wooden. Smaller is better to start with than huge and heavy, as it will take less etheric energy or ectoplasm to move it and producing ectoplasm is a bit like getting any muscle in shape. You want to start small and light-weight.

The number of legs doesn't matter, either. I've done table tipping with a four-legged table with no issues. And square or rectangular works just as well as round.

You either want the table to be large enough or the number of people to be few enough that you all fit around the table without being squished while leaving the table room to move.

Some people recommend cleansing the table to release residual energy attached to it, which you can do by spraying it with salt water and wiping it off or by smudging it with sage smoke. You may also want to say a brief prayer, dedicating the table to Spirit's use. I've also used tables that I used for other things in my home, but it's nice if you can have a dedicated table for table tipping, especially to start.

The room

The room can be lit however you want. Some mediums like it to be completely dark, others do table tipping demonstrations in well-lit auditoriums. I suggest making it dim to start. If it's daytime, draw the shades. If it's night time, have a low lamp on so everyone can see, but without it being too bright. You can have a lit candle nearby and many Spiritualists suggest having a glass or bowl of water in the room to help facilitate communication with Spirit.

Hand placement

Instructions for the placement of your hands varies. Some, such as Bias, advocate for placing the hands palm down, flat on the table, with each person's thumbs touching and their little fingers touching that of the person next to them. In theory, this creates a ring or circuit through which energy can pass from one person to the next. I don't like it, though, and prefer a little space between each person's hands.

I've also done table tipping—and have been instructed by Spirit during a table tipping session—to have our fingertips underneath the table. Listen to your guides and inner knowing.

However you place your hands, keep the pressure as light as you can. You want to make a connection with the table, but not press on it at all.

How to start

When you're ready to start a session, have everyone sit around the table and open with a prayer.

After you've opened with a prayer and asked your guides to step in to help you have a successful and wonderful experience, raise the vibration by singing. Pick songs everyone knows—old standards such as "Row, Row, Row the Boat" are fine, even if you feel silly. Well-known hymns work as well. Sing a few songs, and then sit in meditation and open yourself to the experience.

What to expect

What can you expect to happen? Possibly a number of things.

In *The Art of Mediumship: Psychic Investigation, Clairvoyance and Channeling,* Elaine Kuzmeskus, writes, "With regular practice, your fingers will begin to feel sticky as if they are melding into the table. This is a sure sign that you are making progress. Soon the table should vibrate a bit...With practice, it will move back and forth." (p. 126)

As Bias writes, "In a few moments, the table seems to become 'alive'; those whose hands are on the table can feel an undulation, a sort of pulsation or internal movement in it. Then it moves—it tilts on two or even one leg. It rocks back and forth, it turns in a circle, it slides along the floor." (*Physical Mediumship*, p. 12)

Before the table moves, you should feel a build-up or movement or energy within your solar plexus. If you're the most experienced medium, you may feel a drawing sensation both from and into your solar plexus, as if you are drawing in the etheric energy of the other sitters and using it to create ectoplasm. You may feel a shuddering or vibration in your arms or hands, as if energy is moving through you into the table.

In one experience I had, one of my hands started vibrating and moving, as if it wanted to move the table. In this instance, I consciously relaxed my physical body to let the energy flow through me.

If you're not the most experienced medium in the circle, you may feel a drawing of energy from your solar plexus, either into the table itself or the head medium.

You may also hear raps or creaks coming from the table before it physically moves, tilts or turns. Or you may get the sense of it vibrating.

What to do if nothing happens

If you've said your opening prayer and sung a few songs and nothing seems to be happening here are some things you can try:

- Practice sending energy to the person across the table from you.
- Give the table a physical jiggle or shake—it can be helpful psychologically to know the table can actually move and has not, somehow, become glued to the floor.
- Change your hand placement if that feels right—if your hands were under the table, try putting them on top of the table.
- Relax—notice the tension you're holding in your hands and arms, take a good, deep breath and relax.

- Ask or tell the table to start moving.
- Ask Spirit for instruction—ask your guides or any friendly entities in Spirit for instruction on how to move forward successfully.

What to do when things start happening

When the table starts moving, it's awesome. You'll gasp and laugh. The energy is uplifting and exhilarating. It feels really good. So smile and feel glad within your heart.

Next, it's time to establish a baseline for communication. You can do this in several ways, so choose what feels right for you.

The way I've typically done it is to establish what means *yes* and what means *no*. For instance, clockwise movement means *yes* and counterclockwise rotation means *no*. Or moving to the left and right means one thing and moving up and down—in relation to one of the sitters—means the other. If the table is tilting on two legs, perhaps that can mean *yes*, and if it tilts on the opposite two legs, that can mean *no*. You get the idea.

Some mediums prefer to use the letters of the alphabet to spell out messages, but I think that takes too long and prefer to rely on my mental mediumship to get more detailed or nuanced answers as needed.

Once you've established how you're communicating, you can ask questions—about pretty much anything, always understanding you'll receive only your highest good. You can ask who the Spirit entity is: their name, dates of birth and death, if they were male or female, etc. With yes/no questions, this can require a lot of questions and answers to pin some things down, so decide for yourself what you want to know.

You can also ask questions about your life and your future path. At one table tipping session, I was told I was going to have two more children who'd be twins (I was pregnant with my second child at the time, so I was aghast at this news), but I'd have enough help to cope with it all and my husband would have a good job so we could afford it. I was also told I'd move to the West Coast around the time my oldest was going to Kindergarten. I still have my notes from the session somewhere in one of my many journals where I tucked it afterward.

It turns out I did move to the West Coast when my oldest was four and going into pre-K and I did end up with two more children at the same time—my step-children, who have biological parents of their own to help take care of them, one of whom is their dad who has a good job.

You never know how things are going to turn out, so ask for your highest good and keep your heart and mind open. And take notes.

Levitation

The last of these three ectoplasm-based forms of physical mediumship is levitation. Instances of levitation are much rarer than table tipping and rapping, as it requires more experience and ability with physical phenomena.

In the books I've read, there's not much explanation of how levitation works. By the looks of it, it seems to defy one of the fundamental natural laws: the law of gravity.

Most sources of information about levitation say that it is done through the means of ectoplasm.

Jefts writes, "Ectoplasm…is combined with chemicals and strength drawn from the sitters and the atmosphere and is formed into mosses and rods by the Spirit chemists and placed under the article they desire to levitate." (*The Laws of Spirit Mediumship*, p. 19)

As I have not yet successfully experienced levitation, I can't give you instructions on how to accomplish it. My suggestion is to become adept at table tipping first, then ask Spirit to help you with levitation. Tables have been known to levitate in the air and walk up walls.

My understanding is that it requires a much deeper level of trance than table tipping, so you'll want to also practice trance mediumship to learn how to get yourself into a trance state.

Levitation isn't just for objects. People can levitate, too. In my readings, there are two physical mediums known for their levitation abilities. One was Daniel Douglas Home (1833-1886) who was reported to not only levitate several feet above the ground, but to pass through the window, across the street and through the window of the building across the street. Colin Evans, an early-20th century medium, was also reported to levitate five to seven feet in the air.

Materialization, etherealization and transfiguration

Materialization, etherealization and transfiguration are all stages of the same ectoplasm-based phenomena—the basic difference is how thick and formed is the ectoplasm created in their manifestation.

Basically, each of these phenomena uses ectoplasm to form faces or bodies of those in Spirit.

Transfiguration

Transfiguration, which is sometimes called impersonation, is the easiest to produce of the three phenomena. With this phenomenon a thin layer of ectoplasm forms over the medium's face, allowing them to be transfigured to look like those of loved ones in Spirit.

"In transfiguration, the body of the medium is covered with ectoplasm so that it is transfigured to resemble the form of the manifesting spirit entity." (*Mediumship and Its Phases*, p. 36)

Transfiguration is possible to produce in a home circle, although some mediums seem to have more a talent for it than others. One of my former development circle mates had this talent and, if you kept your eyes open during the meditation, you could see her face change and take on the characteristics of other people. We also purposefully sat for transfiguration at times, with the mediums who wanted to develop the ability taking turns to produce the phenomena and the rest of us acting as batteries and producers of etheric energy to make ectoplasm.

I also attended a transfiguration event with a proficient physical medium in Rochester, New York, and saw this phenomenon occur with my own eyes. It's really quite remarkable to see your loved one's features on someone else's face, and even see the medium gain a different physical appearance, with the suggestion of a female body, if they're male, or to become taller or shorter. It's definitely not a trick of the light or imagination.

In terms of the light, most mediums I know who do transfiguration or materialization work do so in a dimly lit room, usually it with a red light. *Mediumship and Its Phases* instructs that "there must be only enough light for the sitters to witness the phenomenon." (p. 36)

As I've only watched the phenomena and not experienced much of it myself, I can't speak to what it feels like to do it, nor give much in the way of instructions about how to do it. You'd need to be in the company of others, so they can see your face transfiguring if for no other reason, although having others present can also help lend energy to the process. I've also heard of mediums transfiguring, at least partially, as they bring through loved ones in Spirit and taking on some of their features of mannerisms.

When sitting in a circle for transfiguration, my understanding is that the medium is in a trance, at least to some degree. My fellow developing student friend at the time appeared to be in a deep meditation.

As far as what it feels like, expect to have some physical sensations on your face as the ectoplasm forms features over your own. This might feel like your face stretching or becoming tight, or like there's something light and lacy covering your face.

As with all phases of mediumship, begin any sitting for transfiguration by setting the intention to receive only your highest and best good. Meditate and speak with your guides about moving forward in this direction and ask their help throughout the process.

Etherealization

Etherealization is the next step or level beyond transfiguration but not reaching full materialization.

The Laws of Spirit Mediumship describes it as, "materialization to a certain extent, but there are not chemicals enough to form a solid substance of the ectoplasm, it is thin and ethereal and you can see through it." (p. 24)

Materialization

Materialization is considered to be the rarest form of physical phenomena as it takes practice, skill and a certain talent to produce. I haven't ever seen it, or sat for it specifically, so my knowledge is based in what I learned during the course of my studies and further readings.

The Laws of Spirit Mediumship says materialization is "the rarest and most difficult of all phases. Through the instrumentality of the Medium, with the assistance of the Spirit guides and chemists, the Spirit entity is able to manifest in a body which is a replica of its former physical body and is able to walk and talk as when on earth. This body is built of the...vaporous substance called ectoplasm." (p. 24)

Mediumship and Its Phases goes on to explain, "To produce these phenomena, vibrations of the spirit entity wishing to manifest are slowed down by the use of ectoplasm drawn from the medium and sitters until the form becomes visible to our physical eyes. The ectoplasm is molded by the spirit entity through the power of thought until it is solid enough to resemble the former physical body." (p. 37-38)

As with other phases of physical mediumship, the ectoplasm comes from the medium and the sitters. Singing at the start of the session can help raise the vibration in the room in order for the ectoplasm to form into a shape.

A spirit cabinet is often used during materialization to help contain the energy and ectoplasm. The cabinet can be a box made of wood, a partition of curtains, or even a natural alcove in the séance room. The lighting is usually kept dim, "just enough light for the forms to become visible," according to *Mediumship and Its Phases.* (p. 38)

The other important thing to note is not to touch any materialized forms without permission of the medium or their Spirit controls, as that can cause the ectoplasm to retract suddenly into the medium's body, causing pain and potential harm.

If you're going to practice any of these phenomena, from transfiguration to materialization, make sure you're well-grounded before you start, sit in meditation to clear your vibration and center your mind and only practice with others of like mind and like heart. As you connect with Spirit to produce the phenomena, ensure that you remain grounded so you can draw energy from the Earth and from Spirit, rather than use your internal reserves. This is similar to energy healing work, where you must stay connected and grounded, knowing that you're simply a conduit for the energy to move through you, rather than the originator or source of the energy or the healing. In this case, you are the conduit for the manifestation to take place, rather than the source of it, or for the energy needed to create it.

Apportation

Contemporary Definitions of Psychic Phenomena and Related Subjects defines apportation as, "the dematerialization and transporting of an object from one place to another; an apparent penetration of matter by matter."

The objects that dematerialize and then show up in the séance room are called apports.

"Apports are usually small objects, such as flowers or jewelry, that literally appeared out of nowhere and dropped into the laps of the sitters or flew through trumpets onto the floor." (*The Art of Mediumship*, p. 129)

How does this work exactly? Nothing I've read has a firm answer.

The Laws of Spirit Mediumship says that apportation happens, "through the instrumentality of a physical medium, the Spirit Forces are able to pass solid mater through solid matter without injury to either." (p. 35)

Morris Pratt Institute's Educational Course on Modern Spiritualism suggests two hypotheses.

One theory agrees with the above and quotes Nando Fodor's *An Encyclopedia of Psychic Science* in saying that apportation is caused by "the spirits, by an act of willpower, disintegrating the matter to be transported into its molecular elements without altering the form." It goes on to explain that "in this state, the object can pass through the interstices of intervening matter and become reintegrated by a second act of will power." (Lesson 15, p. 13)

This theory is apparently in agreement with the Law of Transmutation of Energy and explains why sometimes apports are either hot or cold when they appear. That could be because passing matter through matter creates friction, which would heat up the object, or because Spirit entities disintegrate a portion of the walls or door to bring the object through, causing it to somehow become cold.

The other theory that Fodor suggests is that the objects go into the fourth dimension—a higher form of space that we're not aware of. If this is the case, "apports are lifted into this dimension, brought to the desired spot and then precipitated into our three-dimensional space." (Lesson 15, p. 13)

It may sound a little wacky, but this second theory rings true for me. When I first started sitting in circles or seances for physical mediumship phenomena, one of the things my teacher taught and we that sat for was apportation. Looking back, it seems that we would have a séance and be open to several different types of physical mediumship happening during its course, whether that was direct voice, materialization, apportation or trance channeling.

I don't recall experiencing apportation during any of those circles, although it does seem that, throughout my life, things have disappeared and reappeared—usually the thing I'm frantically looking for on my way out the door to an appointment. I have a theory about where your missing hairbrushes, car keys, sunglasses and other items go when they momentarily vanish and reappear in the place you know you left them and looked for them.

When I go to look for something and it's not where I left it, I like to say that the Pookas took it. And so I ask the Pookas to put it back. I'm not even sure how I would describe these elusive, mysterious Pookas, but I think of them as other-dimensional beings, who pop in and out of this reality to play with our stuff when we're not using it. They're not mean or harmful in any way, they just like to play. And as you weren't using your car keys, wallet, hair brush or whatever gadget that's not where you left it when you go to look for it, it doesn't hurt to let them borrow it for a bit. Most of the time, it's back where you left it when you need it again. It's only when it's not that there's a problem.

When this happens, I say, literally, out loud in my house (my family is used to me by now), "Hey, Pookas, I need NAME OF THING. Please put it back." Then I walk away from where I know I left it, relax for a moment, go into another part of the house and let go of the idea of it. After a minute, I go back to where I was looking before and there it is, reappeared.

You're probably either laughing at me or shaking your head right now. It's OK. Me and the Pookas—or my idea of them—go way back. It's a harmless, possibly silly belief, and makes me smile when I've lost things, rather than get agitated, so it works for me. You know my motto by now: take what works for you and use it.

Whether there are little furry fourth-dimensional beings who take my stuff when I'm not using it, or not, it does seem that things slip into another dimension from time to time. Reality isn't quite as solid as we'd like to believe.

I think this is how apportation works was well. The Spirit entities you're connecting with can take objects from our third dimension, through space and time in the fourth dimension, and back into our third dimension again. I've read reports of jewelry being transported across the country into a séance room and then identified by its owner as theirs.

If we can connect and communicate with non-physical beings, bringing through evidential information and important messages, why wouldn't this be possible, too?

Precipitation

I'll begin with a confession: I don't know a lot about precipitation in terms of physical mediumship. In the mundane world, precipitation is the stuff that falls from the sky—rain, snow, sleet, hail. As an English person living in the United States in Eugene, Oregon, I'm very familiar with that kind of precipitation.

In terms of physical mediumship, precipitation falls more along the lines of its definition in chemistry: causing a substance to be deposited in solid form from a solution. The solution in this case could be etheric energy or ectoplasm and the solid form often takes the form of paintings or drawings created by Spirit.

Precipitated paintings are works of art on canvas that appear during a séance without anyone in the room actually painting them. Usually, pots of paint and brushes are placed by a blank canvas, which is set somewhere in the séance room. During the course of the séance meditation, Spirit entities paint images and pictures.

The Bangs Sisters were well-known mediums who produced precipitated Spirit paintings in the late

1800s. Many of these are still on display at the Lily Dale Museum at Lily Dale Assembly in New York and at Camp Chesterfield in Indiana. They are said to be in like-new condition more than 100 years after they were created.

If you'd like to learn more about precipitation, read Ron Nagy's book *Precipitated Paintings* and *Portraits from Beyond: The Mediumship of the Bangs Sisters* by N. Riley Heagerty.

Direct voice

When you transition from physical form to Spirit, you give up the use of your physical body. When folks in Spirit want to communicate through voice, there are three ways they tend to communicate through mediumship:

1. By using the sound vibrations in the air (i.e. indirect voice which can be heard through clairaudience)
2. By speaking through a medium in a trance (i.e. channeling)
3. By using a voice box created from ectoplasm and a trumpet to funnel and enhance the sound (i.e. direct voice)

This chapter deals with the last kind—direct voice—which is produced by what we call trumpet mediumship.

Trumpet mediumship

Like materialization, trumpet mediumship is considered to be a challenging and difficult phase of physical mediumship, yet one that can truly convince people of the survival of the Spirit after physical death. There's nothing quite like hearing the voice of a loved one speaking to you again.

How trumpet mediumship works

Trumpet mediumship is an ectoplasmic-based form of physical mediumship. It uses a tool, commonly referred to as a trumpet. It's not anything like the musical instrument we know as a trumpet and you probably couldn't make any noise at all come out through it if you held it up to your mouth and tried to play it.

The trumpet in trumpet mediumship is a lightweight, collapsible aluminum cone, about two to four feet in length. Mine is about 2.5 feet and made up of three sections. Many have a band of glow-in-the-dark tape around the widest end so you can see the trumpet move in the darkened room when you're sitting for direct voice phenomena.

The trumpet does two things to aid in producing this phenomenon—it acts like a little séance cabinet, giving the ectoplasm a container to form in, and it projects the sound, making it louder—a lot like a megaphone.

Direct voice phenomena is produced when the medium's etheric energy becomes ectoplasm and then congeals within the trumpet to form a voice box, which an entity in Spirit can then use to speak words. Materialization is at work here, producing an artificial larynx.

"The communicating spirit, speaking with the ectoplasmic vocal mechanism, causes the air to vibrate and, consequently, sound ensues." (Bias, *Physical Mediumship*, p. 22)

Mediumship and Its Phases says that the Spirit entity learns how to pick up the sound vibrations in the séance room, from the sitters during the course of their singing and conversation, and uses the materialized vocal organs to make words. Because of this, when the sitters sing, it not only helps raise the vibration of the group, but it gives the Spirit entity more sound vibrations to use to speak. (p. 41-43)

The trumpet can also levitate and move around the room. This is also caused by ectoplasmic rods, similar to table tipping and levitation.

How to practice trumpet mediumship

Like with other forms of physical mediumship, it's so helpful to have developed your mental mediumship abilities first. This allows you to hear/see/sense what folks in Spirit are trying to communicate and lets you get guidance from your guides on how to proceed if things feel stuck.

And just like with table tipping, getting raps—either from the trumpet itself or from nearby objects—is often the first sign that phenomena are starting to occur.

The circle

You'll need to form a circle to sit for direct voice phenomena. Bias says you need at least two people—seven to 12 being preferable—with even numbers of males and females, seated alternately in a circle. (*Physical Mediumship*, p. 27) Just do your best. Have at least two people, of whatever genders are interested, and let them sit where they're most drawn.

You should meet regularly, preferably weekly, for about an hour or two, but probably not longer than that. Meet in the same place at the same time each week so that your friends in Spirit, as well as all the attendees, are ready and prepared for the phenomena to occur. The people attending your circle should get there on time and attend as many of the circles as they can. Regularly attendance is important—it shows commitment to the rest of the circle members and to Spirit.

The trumpet

As explained, the trumpet is a light-weight aluminum cone. It's usually collapsible, simply so it's easier to transport—that doesn't add anything to its function as far as I can tell. I purchased mine from the NSAC bookstore in Lily Dale Assembly in New York.

You can place the trumpet on a table in the center of the circle, either on its widest end, horizontally, or on a stand. Sometimes, the medium will hold the trumpet.

The room

Most people who write about trumpet mediumship agree that the room should either be completely dark or lit with only a red light, so as to not disrupt the ectoplasm that forms in the trumpet. There are, however, documented instances of trumpet mediumship, which have been done with subdued or even full light.

You can also try leaving the room dimly lit for the first part of the circle, then darkening it completely when it feels like phenomena are about to happen.

Bias has some specific recommendations, such as using a carpeted room—most likely to reduce unwanted floor creaking from people shifting in their chair—and keeping it at a comfortable temperature and humidity. Use your common sense.

How to start

Get started the same way you would for a table tipping circle. Open with a prayer to set your intention for the circle and follow it with some songs everyone can sing. This raises the vibration of the room and all the people in it, plus it gives folks in Spirit sound vibrations to use to create direct voice phenomena.

Remember that connecting with Spirit is supposed to be enjoyable, even fun. God loves laughter. It's OK to be a little silly. It's OK to even feel silly. Circles are not supposed to be somber affairs. You can be respectful and sincere and be lighthearted at the same time.

Bias recommends alternating "periods of singing and meditative concentration." After which, sitters can share what they experienced and what they're receiving from Spirit. (*Physical Mediumship*, p. 28)

What to expect

While I've sat for direct voice phenomena through trumpet mediumship, I haven't yet been in a circle where it's actually happened. From what I remember, the trumpet did move and levitate in the air, but we didn't get to the point of producing direct voice.

However, from what I've learned, you can expect the trumpet to move and/or raps to emanate from it as the first signs that the phenomena are beginning to occur.

If this happens, consider it a success and keep going. (I think I stopped attending the circle I was in because I was pregnant about subsequently had a baby, which then consumed all my time.)

When you do begin to hear direct voice from someone in Spirit, trust your guides to lead you, and for the voice itself to give you instructions. That sounds like a bizarre suggestion but, once you've made contact with someone from Spirit in this way, no doubt they'll let you know what to do next.

Automatic writing

In the mental mediumship section of this book, I talked about inspirational or inspired writing as a way of demonstrating and developing your claircognizance. Automatic writing is a related phase of mediumship but it falls under the category of physical mediumship.

It's related because you follow the same steps as in inspirational writing—only with automatic writing, you allow yourself to go deeper into a trance state so that Spirit or an entity in Spirit can control the movements of your physical body to produce writing or drawing.

As King writes in *Mediumship and Its Phases*, "Automatic writing comes under physical mediumship and may or may not make use of the consciousness of the medium. The medium's arm is controlled and guided by Spirit; thus the sensitive is not aware of what is being written, but is merely acting as an instrument to convey the thoughts of the spirit sender." (p. 33)

Depending on the depth of the level of trance you're in, you may or may not be conscious of the message that's coming through. In *A Guide to Mediumship and Psychical Unfoldment,* Wallis suggests that the medium may be so unconscious of what's being written that "the mind may be separately engaged in reading or study. In some instances, both hands of the medium are employed simultaneously, and he does not know what has been written until he reads it afterwards." (p. 62)

Bias explains the difference between automatic writing and inspirational writing as, "In inspirational writing, the thought enters the medium's consciousness as he writes, usually at an accelerated pace. In automatic writing, the medium simply holds the pencil in place. The pencil seems to move of its own accord. The medium is not conscious (or only partly so) of what is being written at the time of writing." (p. 14)

Automatic writing seems to be one area of physical mediumship where most people finally agree.

How to practice automatic writing

You can practice automatic writing in a development circle or on your own. Either way, the steps are the same.

You'll need paper and pen or, if you're more comfortable typing, a computer and keyboard. While Spirits of old may not have known how to use a keyboard to type, I think most of them have caught up by now and can figure it out. If that's an easier way for you to communicate, give it a try. I find that it takes less effort for my fingers to type words than to write them, as I'm so used to typing I barely have to think about forming the words with my fingers at the keyboard.

Once you're ready, allow yourself to relax into a trance state, deeper than you did for practicing inspired writing. This may take some time, to really relax and let go of the thoughts and restrictions of your physical body and everyday life. See the chapter on trance channeling for more instruction on achieving a trance state.

In *A Guide to Mediumship and Psychical Unfoldment,* Wallis suggests to "Proceed as though you were speaking to a visible friend, and request that someone will move your hand to write...and...while holding a pencil in readiness, withdraw your thoughts from your hand and arm and assume a passive condition." (p. 173)

You may experience a sense of energy or trembling in your hand or arm, causing the pencil, or your fingers on the keyboard, to move. At first, this may be scribbles and indecipherable words. That's OK. If all that happens is that you produce a bunch of wavy lines, it's actually progress. It may take some time for the entity in Spirit to get used to using your body as its instrument for communicating in this way.

My first attempts at automatic writing produced a whole lot of squiggles across the page and not much else. It felt like the Spirit I was connecting with was learning how to make my body do what it wanted to do, but that it needed some time to learn how to use a physical body again and how to use my particular body. Over time, those squiggles formed words, some of which actually made sense and were useful messages.

Your first attempts may also feel more like inspired writing as you connect with your inner self or even Spirit and become aware of the information that's coming through as you write it. As you continue to practice automatic writing, you'll learn to set aside your conscious mind. You may notice it standing to one side, as a spectator, allowing the flow of information to come through your hands onto the page or screen.

Automatic drawing

Automatic drawing is another form this phenomenon can take. Rather than producing words, you create drawings.

These drawings can range from lovely works of art to undecipherable squiggles. While I don't have direct experience with automatic drawing, my understanding is that it occurs in much the same was as automatic writing. The level of control you're able to give up, as well as the quality of the Spirit entity you connect with, has a lot to do with what you end up producing.

If you're interested in automatic drawing, it may also help to study art and drawing techniques, as your hands and fingers will learn the motions to produce art in the form of drawings, making it easier for the Spirit entity to come through in that way. You wouldn't expect someone in Spirit to teach you how to write from scratch in order to use your hands to produce words, right? You already know how to write. So it can help if you learn how to draw, if you want to produce meaningful automatic drawing phenomena.

Planchette

Another method of developing automatic writing mediumship is to use a planchette or even a Ouija board. I'll go into why Ouija boards aren't creepy later in this section, but first, let's look at the planchette.

A planchette, according to *A Guide to Mediumship and Psychical Unfoldment*, is a mechanical device that can help you produce automatic writing. It's "a heart-shaped little board which has two legs, with wheels at the end, attached to the broader part. Near the pointed end is a hole, into which a piece of pencil is inserted." (p. 176)

To use it, you put a sheet of paper on a table in front of you. Usually one or two people put their hands or fingertips on the upper surface of the board and go into meditation.

"If sitters are sufficiently mediumistic, the instrument will begin to move, slowly at first, but faster and more decidedly later, and probably, after some preliminary strokes, circles, etc., it will settle down as if guided by an unseen hand and begin to write." (p. 177)

Just like all the other phases of mediumship, this takes patience and practice to develop. Once the planchette starts to move, and you get the go-ahead from Spirit, you can ask questions about who you're connecting to and what information they have to communicate.

Similar to table tipping and automatic writing with a pen and paper, you may feel either like the planchette moves of its own accord or that your own arms and hands are vibrating with energy, causing it to move.

Ouija board

You can turn a planchette into a homemade Ouija board by writing the letters of the alphabet, numbers zero to nine and the words Yes and No on a sheet of paper and using a pointer instead of a pencil.

That's basically all a Ouija board is—a way to connect with Spirit and receive information. It doesn't need to be weird or scary at all.

The biggest thing in all forms of mediumship is setting your intention and your boundaries. If you want to use a Ouija board, make sure to ask for your highest good and do it with sincerity. You'll get far different results than if you're drunk and playing party games. Communicating with Spirit isn't a lark. It can be fun, full of light-hearted energy and laughter, but it's not a prank, a trick or a game.

Because of the reputation that Ouija boards have, mediums who wish to use them often purchase or create their own Angel boards.

Using a Ouija board

Bias says that Ouija boards are controversial tools, even among Spiritualists. His take is that what you get depends on the sitters' ability and whether or not you're connecting with Spirit or with your unconscious mind.

"If you decide to experiment with a Ouija Board or planchette, do so in reverent attitude." (*Physical Mediumship*, p. 13) Start with a prayer and ask your Spirit guides to join you.

"Then relax, sit back, calmly and confidently wait until you feel within yourself that your guide has responded as is now within your aura." Some mediumship teachers call this feeling Sitting in the Power.

At that point, place your hands on the little table or platform on the board and allow your hands to move where they are lead, the same way you would using a planchette. Bias recommends having two people with both hands on the platform, a they'll get better results than one person.

Because of its reputation, most NSAC Spiritualist churches recommend against using Ouija boards. In fact, they recommend against using any tools at all for producing mediumship, including Tarot cards and pendulums. This is mostly because these tools can become crutches, with your energy focused on the tools, rather than your connection with Spirit. Use them, perhaps as a starting point.

Like I tell all my students, ultimately you have to figure out your own truth and your own path. Go into it setting your intention for your highest good, and with a sense of curiosity and wonder, and know you'll experience exactly what you're supposed to right in this present moment.

Independent writing

Independent writing is also known as slate writing. It's a type of physical mediumship that produces writing or drawing on slates or paper without using the medium's hands. Instead, Spirit entities use ectoplasm to move the drawing tools, or precipitate them directly onto the surface of the paper or slate.

According to *The Laws of Spirit Mediumship,* "The slate writer is a physical medium the same as the automatic writer, but the medium does not do the writing, the Spirit does this by use of ectoplasm drawn from the body of the medium." (p. 32)

Sometimes sitters will hear scratching sounds during the séance indicating that writing or drawing is taking place on the slates.

This form of mediumship isn't practiced much today and is as rare as other precipitated or ectoplasm-based phenomena.

How to practice slate writing

I've never sat for independent writing, but here's the procedure as I understand it.

First, you'll need something for the Spirit entities to write on. People don't tend to use slates anymore, as our classrooms have advanced well beyond slates and chalk. However, you can use cards or sheets of paper.

Most instructions I've found recommend either covering the pieces of slate, card or paper—with or without a pencil enclosed between them—in dark cloth or a box, or conducting the sessions in a darkened room. This sets up the right environment for ectoplasm to form, provided you believe that ectoplasm can only be formed in the dark. Given that you'll probably be new to producing ectoplasmic phenomena, you may want to do everything you can to encourage the process. And, while the phenomena can apparently be produced whether or not there's any kind of drawing implement with the paper or slates, you might as well include some, just in case it helps.

Sometimes the medium will hold the slates or paper in their hands during the meditation or séance. Other times they're placed nearby on a table. If you want to make sure no one is fiddling with things—although hopefully you're doing this work with people you trust in an atmosphere of willingness and curiosity, rather than skepticism—you can mark the paper in some way to make sure it's still the same paper when you look at it later.

The Art of Mediumship describes Victorian Spiritualists sitting for independent writing, putting two clean slates with a piece of chalk between them in a sealed, light-proof box, which is then placed on the center of the séance table.

"Then the physical medium who usually sat at the head of the table went into trance, while the group meditated. Within moments, the sound of chalk scratching across the slates was heard by all present. When the sealed slates were opened, messages, sometimes in several languages, or even pictures were on the slates." (p. 47)

For more information about independent writing, read Ron Nagy's *Slate Writing: Invisible Intelligences.*

Trance channeling

Trance channeling is physical mediumship? Yes, it is. Here's why.

When you are truly channeling an entity in Spirit, you're in a state of trance. If you're still in control of your mind and body, you're not channeling—you're in a state of inspiration, which is related to claircognizance and uses your mental faculties, rather than your physical body. This is similar to how inspired writing and automatic writing are related, but classified differently. Inspired writing comes through claircognizance; automatic writing is a form of physical mediumship.

The Laws of Spirit Mediumship describes it this way: "In trance, the mind and personality of the medium are entirely submerged, the Spirit taking full control of the instrument and the medium is unconscious of all that is said or done. In inspiration, the medium is full conscious and in perfect control of mind and body." (p. 31)

Channeling can take different forms, from a light to a deep trance state—and the difference in the level of trance determines whether or not you're truly channeling Spirit or are in an inspired state. Just as with inspired writing, a lot of good can come out of inspirational speaking and connecting with Spirit through claircognizance. But it's not the same as trance channeling.

There's more confusion surrounding channeling as well—the type of entity that you're connecting to. As you'll know if you've read *Led by Light, Book 1,* I have a different take on Spirit guides than a lot of people. My understanding, direct from my own guides and confirmed with fellow mediums, is that the entities we typically call Spirit guides aren't separate entities from us. Rather, they're aspects of our own higher self that we give personality and characteristics to in order to be able to connect with and relate to them. When I read about channeling and connecting with guides, I often wonder if these guides are truly separate excarnate entities, or really the person's higher self. I happen to think my higher self is awesome and I'm quite happy to have a chat with it on a regular basis. I think we're so much greater as spiritual beings than we give ourselves credit for and that it's easier to say that these entities are separate from us when, really, they're not.

It may also be possible to communicate with non-physical beings who have never taken human form or who are from planets other than ours, and who may act as guides to us in various ways. However, I think the majority of what we call Spirit guides—channeled or not—is actually an aspect of our own higher self.

Why is this important in terms of trance channeling? Because trance channeling is a form of physical mediumship—which means it's a way of communicating with spiritual beings who are not part of your higher self. These entities must be able to manipulate or effect the medium's mind in order to control their nervous system and physical body.

"To take control, the spirit enters the aura of the medium and blends with it. In this way, the mind of the spirit can influence the mind, brain and nervous system of the entranced medium. Thus, any control a spirit guide exercises upon a medium is purely mental. No spirit can take possession of the sitter's physical body." (*Mediumship and Its Phases*, p. 21)

My understanding of how this occurs is that, during deepening meditation and relaxation, you connect with your master guide (which is part of your higher self) as you go into a trance state. Your guide oversees the process of allowing Spirit to step into your auric field and stimulate your brain and nervous system, thereby allowing your body to speak and move under the Spirit entity's direction.

The amount of control the Spirit entity has over your body is directly related to the level of trance that you're in. *The Art of Mediumship* describes the different brain waves that come into play during mediumship. We live mostly in a Beta brain wave state, in our everyday lives. Mental mediumship, however, is done in the Alpha state, while trance mediumship occurs during the Theta and Delta states.

"At first, Spirit will stand behind the medium. Then, with practice, the guide will blend with the aura of the medium more and more until the guide overshadows the medium. This is the most common level of trance. The medium is conscious, but also aware spirit is talking through him...In the final stage, the medium will leave their body and the guide will enter." (*The Art of Mediumship*, p. 134)

How to practice trance channeling

There are two main steps involved in practicing trance channeling: having a solid relationship with your master Spirit guide and being able to relax into a trance state.

Your master Spirit guide

You must have complete confidence and trust in your guides to do trance work. To develop that, you need to spend time with them during meditation. And, as your Spirit guides are really part of your higher self, it helps a whole lot to have a good relationship with yourself.

Whatever you need to do to make that happen—being able to say, "I love you," to yourself in the mirror without cringing, practicing self-compassion, setting and maintaining your boundaries in your everyday and spiritual life—I encourage you to do it. Don't use mediumship to escape your relationship with yourself. Learn to like and support yourself in this life. Live in integrity. It'll make the rest of your work so much easier.

Your master Spirit guide is the head honcho, the one who's closest to you and oversees the rest. They're the leader of your Spirit band. Get to know this guide—learn their name, personality, the role they play for you. The best way to do this is through meditation and quiet reflection. Take the time to build this relationship until it's one of utmost trust.

Getting into a trance state

Relaxation is key when entering into a trance state deep enough to channel. Since you'll usually be speaking or writing while in trance, sit up to do your relaxation exercises, rather than lie down.

Not every relaxation and self-hypnosis method works for everyone. I'll suggest a couple here for you to try, if you're so inclined, but feel free to try others if these don't feel quite right for you.

In general, to get into a trance state, you want to first relax your body and then allow your mind to relax and go into slower brain wave frequencies, through the Alpha state, into Theta, and possibly Delta states.

Make sure that you're in a quiet place where you won't be disturbed before you do these exercises. Being interrupted from the deep relaxation needed for trance can be jarring and even painful. Turn off your phone, close the door, dim the lights and allow yourself to be in a sacred space while you do this work.

As you begin, start with an opening prayer, affirming that you'll receive only your highest and best good and asking your master Spirit guide to step in with you to assist in the process of connecting with a guide or entity in Spirit that you can then channel. When I was working on trance mediumship, it was as a student in a development circle, which allowed me to draw on others' energy, presence and guidance.

Relaxing your body

Progressive relaxation is a great way to relax your body—and it can be done in several ways.

One technique involves tightening and releasing your muscles, from your toes to your forehead, going slowly through each muscle group. Beginning with your toes and your feet, tighten them and hold them in an active state for a few seconds on your inhale, then release them on your exhale. Move on to your ankles and calves, then your knees, thighs, buttocks and pelvis, up your abdomen and back, to your shoulders, neck, jaw, face, eyes and forehead. The process of holding the muscles tightly then releasing them allows them to fully relax.

Another technique uses visualization rather than actively using your muscles. This is the technique I've used for years to help my children relax into sleep when they have difficulty letting go of the worries of the day behind them and the day ahead. It's a method my first yoga teacher taught me when I was in my late teens. In this case, you won't be trying to fall asleep, but it can still bring deep relaxation to the body.

Again, begin with your feet. Imagine soft, relaxing energy enveloping your feet. Say to yourself, *relaxed feet, quiet feet, warm feet, gentle feet, relax.* This energy then moves up into your ankles as, in your mind, you say, *relaxed ankles, slow, quiet, warm ankles, relax*.

Continue moving up your body, addressing each body part: your knees, thighs, hips and pelvis, lower and upper abdomen, lower back, upper back, chest, shoulders, arms, elbows, forearms, wrists and hands, neck, jaw, face, eyes, ears, forehead and scalp. Speak to each part of yourself in turn, giving it direction and permission to be relaxed, quiet, soft and gentle. Imagine warm, relaxing energy moving up through your body as you do this, enveloping you in its safe embrace.

Your body should feel heavy and relaxed, as if you can't move your limbs or open your eyelids because they are too heavy and solid.

Relaxing your mind

Once your body is relaxed and still, move onto your mind. I end my progressive body relaxation exercise with, *mind relax, relax, relax*.

Beyond just that directive, there are several methods to allow your mind to go deeper down into the state needed for trance mediumship.

One method is to imagine yourself climbing down a ladder. With each exhale, climb down a rung of the ladder. With each rung you descend, your mind goes deeper into relaxation, down, down, down. The effect of imagining your mind dropping puts you into a trance state. You can also use steps, an elevator or escalator to move downwards. This is similar to the idea of going up a staircase to meet your Spirit guide, just in the opposite direction to allow your mind to achieve deep relaxation.

You don't need to think while you're doing this exercise beyond being aware of your inhalation and exhalation and seeing yourself go down a step or rung with each out breath and feeling yourself descend.

At some point, you'll notice a difference in your body and in the space around you. Things will feel quieter, you may hear or sense a buzzing or humming, and it may seem like you're either in a much bigger space or like you have a box over your head.

When you're ready to come out of this state, wiggle your fingers or toes. This will draw your awareness back into your physical body. While you may seem so relaxed that you feel you can't move, you still retain control over your body. You can still move it and take care of it—and it has its own intelligence and willpower to stay alive and take care of you.

But before you do, ask Spirit to step in to communicate through you.

Asking Spirit to step in

Here's my confession for this chapter: I'm not a successful trance medium. I've studied it and practiced it briefly. I've sat in development for it and have felt Spirit overshadow my energy and begin to take control of my body's faculties. And that's as far as I got.

It turns out, that's fairly common.

To get to this point, I did the work to get into a light trance state and then invited Spirit it, through my guide, to speak and communicate through me.

I felt my sense of self step back and to the side, almost as if I was watching myself. And I felt another energy—that wasn't mine—feel out my body, as if it was getting used to it and figuring out how it worked. I felt sensations in my arms and chest and a strong desire to cough and clear my throat.

I did not, however, start speaking. Looking back years later, I realize I felt intimidated, as a fairly new medium in my mentor's exclusive mediumship circle. I didn't want to seem like I was showing off, sitting for trance mediumship for a couple of weeks and then just doing it, and I also didn't want to make a fool of myself. I was also possibly a little too independent and headstrong to give up control of my physical body to another entity, especially one I didn't initially know well. I didn't feel comfortable ceding control of it to someone in Spirit. I figured if they wanted to express themselves in a physical body, they could incarnate and get their own, as I was using mine! If you feel this way when talk of channeling comes up, I want you to know it's OK. This isn't a required thing for you to do.

If the idea of channeling Spirit sounds totally awesome to you, that's fine, too. I encourage people to listen to the voice within them and follow the path of their own highest good.

If I was in the same situation now, I'd allow myself to relax some more and begin speaking. One trance mediumship suggestion is to just begin speaking whatever words want to come out of your mouth without thinking about it. Those first words are the hardest, just as they are in automatic writing. Once the flow of words starts going, it gets easier to keep them going and Spirit naturally steps in. The energy then flows.

If you're going to practice trance channeling, it's a good idea to have someone with you to record what you say and to lend their loving energy and support to you during the experience. A development circle is even better, especially one with an experienced teacher to guide you.

I think there's definitely some wonderful information from Spirit that we receive through channeling and it certainly has its uses and place in the world of mediumship.

Spirit photography

When people think about Spirit photography, there are two things that usually come to mind. One is skotography—Spirit communication via an instrument outside the medium's body, such as photographic paper. The other is capturing images of Spirit on film.

One of these—skotography—is a form of physical mediumship; the other isn't. But it's a common phenomenon and pretty cool so, while skotography will be the focus of the chapter, I'll include some information about the other form of Spirit photography, as well.

The Laws of Spirit Mediumship describes skotography phenomena as, "A physical phase of mediumship giving one the power to produce faces and forms of Spirit loved ones on a sensitive plate or film, thus producing a Spirit picture. It's a very rare phase." (p. 35)

It's considered a form of physical mediumship as it uses a medium's physical energies to produce images from Spirit. I haven't read any explanations of how it's done, but Spirit using ectoplasm to manipulate the chemical structure of the photographic substance seems the most likely method.

Any kind of photographic paper of film can be used. The Scole Group produced Spirit images on rolls of unopened film. When they were developed, there were photos of people and places that were confirmed as authentic, as well was writing and drawings.

In times past, when we still took our photos on light-sensitive film, that's what people used for Spirit photography. However, there's not so much of that around anymore, and most of us barely even remember how to get film developed. You could also potentially use light-sensitive paper, like the kind you use to make sun prints. Keep whatever light-sensitive material away from light, perhaps in a sealed envelope or box, until you're ready to get it developed or see what's come through from Spirit.

During meditation, place the light-sensitive material on the physical medium's solar plexus, heart or forehead and ask Spirit to affect it. There's no set amount of time you need to leave the light-sensitive material in place—follow your guides' instruction and your own intuition.

I haven't tried this form of mediumship, but I think it'd be interesting to practice during a development circle using sun-sensitive paper that doesn't need any special chemicals to develop.

Capturing Spirit on camera

People interested in communicating with Spirit will often find orbs, ghost lights and rods in their photos. These seem to show up in family photos and in places where it's likely for Spirit to be present, such as cemeteries and churches.

While it's true that these kinds of images are easy to manipulate, either digitally or by altering film negatives, I've seen so many orbs in my own photography that I know they're a genuine phenomenon.

Spirit orbs, rods and the like aren't a phase of mediumship, either mental or physical, but they are interesting and so I'm including them here briefly.

Orbs show up as spheres, often very detailed with many facets, and sometimes containing a face. They are different than flecks of dust or raindrops.

Ghost lights and rods show up as streaks of light or a stick that sometimes twirls or bends. If you think you've captured some of these, just make sure it's not your camera strap!

Vortices are funnel shapes, which sometimes can move around when captured on video camera.

Ectoplasm, as previously described, shows up as a translucent to thick white fog, mist or cloud.

Most Spirit lights and orbs show up by happy accident. In my photos, they've most often occurred during special family events, such as Christmastime or weddings, or at places with lots of Spirit about, like at the Lily Dale Assembly auditorium.

If you want to capture some intentionally, here are a few tips to get you started.

- Choose a location that you sense has Spirit presence or energy.
- Use a camera with a high resolution (whatever that is at the current moment of technological innovation). Your smartphone camera is probably fine.
- Say a prayer of intention, asking to receive your highest good and for Spirit to step in to be photographed.

- Take photos wherever you sense there may be Spirit present. Trust yourself.
- If it's dark, use the flash, or use an infrared camera.

When you're done, thank Spirit. You're most likely to see Spirit orbs and lights once you look at the photos either zoomed in on your phone or on a computer monitor.

Dowsing

These final two chapters are devoted to a couple of phenomena that aren't always considered physical mediumship, but which I feel deserve some space and thought—dowsing/pendulum and spoon bending.

In both phenomenon, your own mind and body come into play—you tune into your inner self and the wisdom that resides there, rather than connecting with a separate physical entity. There's no ectoplasm making the pendulum move or Spirit entities coming through your body in the form of automatic writing or trance channeling. Yet there's something very interesting going on that, if you connect to it, can help build your trust with Spirit and your higher self and help your conscious mind get past its limiting beliefs.

Dowsing has been practiced for centuries, often to discover natural resources, such as water. When you think of dowsing, you may think of a Y-shaped stick, held with both hands on the forked part. That's one way of dowsing. Today, dowsing is most often practiced using a pendulum.

Pendulums have been used for eons as a way of connecting with Spirit and divining answers to our myriad of questions as we navigate this human experience. They're simple to use and a way to connect with your intuition.

How pendulums work

Divination using a pendulum really isn't all that mysterious. The answers come from within your inner, wiser self (hello, intuition!). It's connected to your ideomotor response, a mind-body connection that causes slight muscular movements independent of your conscious desires or emotions.

Skeptics think of the ideomotor response as an unconscious reaction to a stimulus and use this explanation to disregard tools such a pendulums or phenomena like automatic writing and table tipping. However, I consider it to be a mind-body connection that taps into your intuition to give you signals that can be translated into clearer answers using a pendulum. Intuition uses your body all the time to give you information—a sinking feeling in your stomach, a tug in your gut, the rising of your heart with inspiration or excitement.

A pendulum is just a tool to interpret these body sensations. The trick here is that you need to detach your emotions and expectations from the answers you receive so that you can access your intuition and higher self.

What to use as your pendulum

You can use many different things as pendulums—any slightly weighted object can work. You could use a rock, crystal, pendant or ring, for example. Hang it from a chain, string or ribbon—something that allows it to hang straight and move easily. The chain should be 4-15" long—whatever feels right to you. Many people like to purchase a crystal pendulum with a chain to use specifically for work with Spirit; others are happy using a necklace or putting a special ring on a chain. As long as it hangs straight and moves easily and evenly, it should work.

How to hold and use your pendulum

When you begin working with a pendulum, do so in a quiet, peaceful place. Whether that's the middle of the woods or your living room is up to you. But you should be free from distractions and interruptions.

Hold the chain between your thumb and forefinger with your writing hand, letting the weighted part hang. Relax your hand and fingers.

Before setting up communication with your pendulum—which you'll want to check each time you use it, not just the first time—give yourself a moment to settle yourself and get centered. Take some deep breaths, allow yourself to set aside the cares and worries you usually carry around with you, and connect with Spirit. Ask for your highest and best good and trust that's what you'll receive.

Setting up communication with your pendulum

Before you can ask Spirit questions via your pendulum, you need to learn how your pendulum will communicate with you. There are a few ways to do this which are outlined below.

Tell it what you want yes and no to be

Deliberately move the pendulum in clockwise circles or backwards and forwards and ask it to always indicate a *yes* or a positive response with that movement.

Then deliberately move the pendulum in anti-clockwise circles or side to side and ask it to use that movement to indicate a *no* or a negative response.

Similarly, you can use a printed pendulum chart with responses indicated on it and instruct your pendulum to use that to communicate with you.

Some pendulums are responsive to this. Others appear to have resistance to being told what to do and want to use their own method.

Ask the pendulum

Ask your pendulum to show you *yes* and *no* and wait to see how it swings each time. First, ask for *yes* and wait, allowing the pendulum to swing as it will. Then ask for *no* and wait until you get a response.

You can also ask questions with yes/no answers—questions you already know the answer to, that are solid, objective and grounded in reality. Like: *Is it Wednesday today? Is it daytime? Is my name legal name currently Joanna?* All questions you ask your pendulum need to be specific—for instance, my soul name isn't Joanna, and my legal name hasn't always been Joanna. But it is currently, and my pendulum will answer yes to that.

Another way is to visualize a happy or successful moment in your life or feeling within yourself. I like to imagine my children or partner hugging me and telling me, "I love you." The pendulum will respond to this positive emotion with a *yes* response. Then remember a time of sadness, sorrow or deep disappointment. The pendulum will respond to this different emotion with its movement for *no*.

For some people, when the pendulum swings left to right (like the shaking of your head), it means *no*. When it swings backward and forward (like nodding your head) it means *yes*. Swinging in a circular movement means uncertainty: *maybe, not now, ask again later*. But the pattern might be different for you. A clockwise motion may mean *yes*, while counterclockwise may mean *no*. That's why you start with some objective questions to determine how your pendulum will give answers and information.

Trust your intuition here. There are times I've asked a question and have received a weak response from the pendulum and have heard within myself that I didn't phrase the question specifically enough or that it's information I don't need to know right now.

Using your pendulum

Now that you've got your pendulum set up with whichever method that works for you, you can begin using it.

There's probably no limit to what you can use a pendulum for—basically anything you can ask questions about. Here are some of the major areas that people use often pendulums for.

Finding something that's lost

Pendulums can be very helpful in finding lost items, people and pets. How you use it depends on how narrow or wide the scope of where you're looking is.

In a room

Ask the pendulum where the object is located. The pendulum will swing in its direction. Move in that direction and notice if and how the pendulum changes. Keep going until you find the item.

You can also do this in conjunction with clairsentience, feeling where the object is as a tug in your gut, or tapping into your clairvoyant abilities and seeing where the item is. Often, as you ask the pendulum to lead you to the object, you'll receive information about it through your intuitive senses as well.

In a house

Go through your house, room by room or in your mind, and ask the pendulum, *is the object is in this room?* You'll receive a *yes* or *no* response for each room.

Once you've narrowed it down to a specific room, go into that room and ask where the object is located.

On a map

You'll need a map for this. It doesn't matter, as far as I can tell, if it's a paper map you can fold out flat or a map you pull up on your smartphone or tablet. But you want to be able to hold the pendulum over it.

Ask the pendulum if the object is in the area of the map. You'll get a yes or no answer. If yes, point to places on the map, or zoom into it if it's on a digital display, to narrow down the location. You may also feel the pendulum tug or pull toward a specific location, which is why it's helpful to have it on a flat surface.

If you're looking for a person or pet, it can be helpful to have a photo or object of belonging to the person to tune into their energy frequency.

Making decisions

A pendulum can be used to find answers to anything you can ask a yes/no question about. *Will I live until I'm 120? Should I move to Hawaii? Does my cat have cancer?*

Prepare your question in advance, either in your mind or by writing it down. Get clear and calm within yourself (meditation is great for this), then ask your question. Allow your mind to relax and empty and wait for the pendulum's response.

It turns out that there are a whole lot of things about this life I don't want to know the answers to ahead of time. Do you really want to know when you're going to die? Or if your kids will grow up healthy and give you grandkids? Or if your latest book will be a best seller? I think there are some things we're supposed to find out as we go along—not try and skip ahead in the book of our lives to find out how it all works out. But you have free will and may feel differently.

Choosing between several options

You can also use your pendulum to get information from Spirit if there are several things you're trying to choose between—such as houses you're looking at purchasing, supplements you're thinking of taking, people you're thinking of marrying, anything that has more than 1 or 2 choices.

Set out the various options, or representations of them, such as a photo, on a flat surface. Hold your pendulum over each option, moving very slowly. Wait to feel a downwards tug or pull over one of the options. The pendulum may also feel very heavy before it tugs. Keep going over all the options until you've moved over all of them—you may feel a tug on more than one, so you want to discern which has the strongest pull.

Connecting with Spirit

Your pendulum can also be used as a tool to activate your mental mediumship abilities.

By holding a pendulum over an object, you may be able to tune into it with psychometry and begin to receive stronger impressions with your intuitive senses, perhaps seeing, hearing, or feeling information about the object and its former owner(s).

You can also use a pendulum to connect with Spirit entities in a place, especially if you feel like there's a Spirit presence around. You can use the pendulum in its many ways—to locate where the Spirit is in a room, building or area, to ask questions of the Spirit, and as a magnifier of your intuitive senses to get clearer information about it.

Using a pendulum in this way does several things. First, it helps you connect in with your inner self, allowing you to access your intuitive self, which is what you need to open and use your clairsenses. Second, it's a tool, which can give you confidence. It seems easier for many people to trust a tool, whether that's a pendulum, a tarot card deck or anything external to them, than it is to simply trust themselves and the information they get. Lastly, the crystal structure of the pendulum itself can help to focus and magnify energy. When I do phone sessions with clients, I'll often hold a quartz rod to amplify the energy and make a more solid connection to my client and their loved ones in Spirit. I don't technically need it but, especially if the energy feels low for some reason, it definitely helps. Plus gems are pretty and feel good.

Things to keep in mind

If you're not getting satisfying results using your pendulum, here are some things to keep in mind as you work with it.

Maintain emotional detachment from the outcome

If you're getting confusing or contradicting answers, take an emotional step back. The pendulum allows you to make full use of your combined conscious and unconscious knowledge. But you need to disconnect from what you think you want. Ask for your highest good and let go of the answer itself.

The best frame of mind to be in is one of childlike innocence, expectancy and wonder.

This can be understandably hard, as you wouldn't be asking questions if you didn't care about the answer. But it's vital to let go of expectations and do what you need to get into a quiet, centered place before doing pendulum work.

Ask specific questions

Sometimes the answers still don't come clearly. If so, ask clarifying questions. You may not be phrasing your question clearly.

I've found that you need to ask specific questions that can't be interpreted in multiple ways. Those get the strongest, clearest responses.

Accept you may not be supposed to know

There are things you're not supposed to know right now.

Your intuition works right here in the present. It shines the light of Spirit on the very next steps on your path—because those are the only steps you can actually take. You can't walk on your path of a year from now, only on your path today. So perhaps knowing if you'll be in a different job or house or with a different partner one, five or 10 years from now isn't something you truly need to know (although it may be something you want to know).

Trust that, if you've asked for your highest good, that's what you're receiving.

Spoon bending

Spoon bending is a form of psychokinesis—the ability to manipulate matter using your mind. Many forms of physical mediumship fall under the label of psychokinesis as, while the information isn't coming through your mind, you do use your mind to control your body to produce physical mediumship phenomena.

I'm not sure if spoon bending is truly physical mediumship, but I'm including it here because it's an excellent way to learn to let go of limiting beliefs. Once you've felt a solid metal spoon get soft and easily bend through the power of your thought and intention, it tends to open you mind to new possibilities. If you can do that, what else can you do?

The basics of spoon bending are this: you concentrate your energy on a metal spoon and, when it suddenly feels soft and pliable, you bend and twist the spoon with little resistance until it begins to get hard to move again. In theory, you can make the spoon bend without using any physical force at all. But even using your hands, you can feel a clear difference in the strength of the spoon and its ability to bend easily.

It requires a willingness to let go of your belief that spoons are solid, non-bending objects (or that they require a great deal of physical force to bend), and the ability to feel the energy of the spoon so that you know when to bend it.

How to practice spoon bending

There are several methods you can use to bend spoons. The most important thing is to get out of your own way and allow it to happen.

First, get a spoon you don't mind bending. I like to get spoons and forks from thrift stores for spoon bending. Choose a spoon that's not so thin and weak you can easily bend it with just muscle strength, but not so incredibly thick that you need tools to bend it.

Find a comfortable spot where you won't be disturbed. Take a deep breath in. Then let it out. Know that only your highest and best good will come to you. Set your intention: "I will bend this spoon."

Hold the spoon in both your hands. Flex it a little and feel the natural resistance of the metal. Then do any of the following exercises until the spoon is ready to bend.

You'll know your spoon is ready to bend when it feels pliable. The metal will soften and become like taffy. Ever seen hard candy being made? When it's at a certain temperature, it's soft and pliable, able to be stretched. But when it cools, it sets, becoming hard. The spoon will feel like that. It'll get soft for a moment or two, maybe a few seconds, then it'll firm up again.

Counting (and breathing)

Decide that, when you get to 10, the spoon is going to bend for you.

Inhale 1. Exhale 2.

Inhale 3. Exhale 4.

Inhale 5. Exhale 6.

Inhale 7. Exhale 8.

Inhale 9. Exhale 10, applying a little pressure to the spoon. It's ready to bend when it feels pliable and soft.

If it doesn't want to give, that's OK. Keep breathing. If it does bend, keep bending and twisting it for as long as it feels soft. Then stop and take a look.

Getting excited

Some people like to command the spoon to bend. As you hold the spoon and breathe slowly and deeply, say, "Bend, spoon, bend!" You can repeat this several times until the spoon becomes pliable.

You can also try jumping up and down to raise your energy. Or even shouting. (I don't like shouting at spoons myself, but it works for some folks.)

Singing to the spoon

Do you know the tune, "Sun, sun, Mr. golden sun, please shine down on me?" Sometimes I like to sing to my spoon: "Spoon, spoon, Mr. bendy spoon, please will you bend for me?"

It sounds ridiculous, but it works. The combination of song and the silliness of it raises my vibration—and that of the spoon—and distracts me enough to allow the spoon to bend.

Realize that everything is energy

My most successful way of bending spoons is knowing that everything in this world is made up of energy. It just vibrates at different frequencies. The spoon is more solid than I am. But it doesn't have to be. People in Spirit are less solid than I am, but I raise the frequency of my vibration and use my intuitive senses to be able to sense them and communicate with them.

Hold the spoon in both hands. Become aware of the energy of your own body. Feel the energy of your aura, right around your body, close to it.

Extend your energy to the spoon. Allow the spoon to become infused with your energy.

Know that we are all one, from the same source energy, all connected.

Know that just as you can bend the fingers of your hand, so too can you bend the spoon. Imagine it as part of your body, part of your hand.

Then bend it.

You can also imagine the distance between the protons and electrons in the spoon's atoms increasing. This makes it pliable and easy to bend.

The benefits of spoon bending

Beyond creating cutlery that's no longer good for its original intended use, spoon bending does a few things for me:

- It helps me focus my energy. I can only bend spoons when I'm in a quiet, focused frame of mind.
- It reminds me that we're all energy and that all energy is connected.
- I feel connected to Spirit.
- It makes me ponder what else is possible. When I'm having a hard moment or something feels too difficult to surmount, I look at my twisted-up cutlery and think, "Huh, well, that wasn't impossible. I did that. I can do this too."

I took my kids to a spoon-bending workshop once (because they'll learn things from other people so much better than they'll learn them from their own mother), and they had a great experience. This is what my son, who was 10 at the time, said about it.

"At first, it was difficult and frustrating because I couldn't do it. But then as soon as I did it once, it felt like I could do it another time and another time and another time and it was really fun."

"It felt like a hard object at first before I bent the spoon. Then as I bent the spoon

it felt 20 times weaker and then it just went flop and I could bend it. I felt very accomplished."

Consider how you might feel on your journey once you know that seemingly impossible things are actually quite possible. Give yourself the freedom to move forward on your path, trusting in Spirit and in yourself.

Resources

This book would not have been possible without the help of several others.

Some of these books are available online and in bookstores, others may need to be special-ordered from places such as the National Spiritualist Association of Churches bookstore (a book list is available online).

Following is a list of books cited in this text. For those that may be difficult to find, I've noted the publisher.

Marilyn Awtry, *Contemporary Definitions of Psychic Phenomena and Related Subjects*, publisher: National Spiritualist Association of Churches

Rev. Joanna Bartlett, *Led by Light: How to develop your intuitive mediumship abilities, Book 1, Unfolding* (2016)

Rev. Joanna Bartlett, The Spiritual Symbols Workbook: Create your personal dictionary of intuitive, metaphysical and psychic symbols (2016)

Rita S. Berkowitz and Deborah S. Romaine, *The Complete Idiot's Guide to Communicating with Spirit* (2003)

Clifford Bias, *Physical Mediumship* (2000), publisher: Universal Spiritualist Association

Rev. Lena Barnes Jefts, *The Laws of Spirit Mediumship* (2007) publisher: National Spiritualist Association of Churches

Nandor Fodor, *An Encyclopedia of Psychic Science* (1969)

Margaret L. Kind, *Mediumship and Its Phases* (2002) publisher: National Spiritualist Association of Churches

Elaine Kuzmeskus, *The Art of Mediumship: Psychic Investigation, Clairvoyance and Channeling* (2012)

M.H. and E. W. Wallis, *A Guide to Mediumship and Psychical Unfoldment*, publisher: Health Research, www.healthresearchbooks.com

Additional recommended books

These books may also assist you in developing your mental and physical mediumship skills

Robin P. Foy, *In Pursuit of Physical Mediumship*

Ron Nagy, *Precipitated Paintings*

Ron Nagy, *Slate Writing: Invisible Intelligences*

Other resources

Physicalmediumship4u.ning.com – a free membership-based website offering help and advice from experts in the field.

Index

M

N

O

P

R

S

T

V

Acknowledgements

I wouldn't know much at all about physical mediumship without the development circles that sprang from Plymouth Spiritualist Church in Rochester, NY, the mother church of modern Spiritualism and my home church.

I have fond memories of sitting together with other mediums, learning table tipping, trumpet mediumship, transfiguration and other forms of physical mediumship. The thing I remember most was the fun we had when Spirit came through!

I'm also grateful to my guides, who are always there to make sure I don't get into too much trouble with my ever-present curiosity.

About the Author

Rev. Joanna Bartlett is an ordained Spiritualist minister and certified medium with the National Spiritualist Association of Churches. Originally from England, she lives in the lovely West Coast town of Eugene, Oregon, with her naturally cheerful husband and blended family of four children. There, she teaches classes and circles on mediumship and intuition development, writes books, and see clients and mentors students across the country.

Learn more about her and her work at www.alightintuition.com where you can subscribe to her mailing list, watch YouTube videos and read blog posts about intuition and mediumship development. You can also connect with her on Facebook and Instagram.

As an independently-published author, it'd mean a whole lot to her if you'd review this book on Amazon, Goodreads or wherever you fancy, so that other people can know what to expect and whether they should buy and read it themselves.

Printed in Great Britain
by Amazon